DEPLOYABLE SECURITY TRAINER
For Security Professionals in the Combat Environment

OCTOBER 2012

DEPLOYABLE SECURITY TRAINER | OCTOBER 2012

TABLE OF CONTENTS

TABLE OF CONTENTS

TABLE OF CONTENTS

1.1   INITIAL BRIEFING

All personnel should receive an initial briefing from the activity security office.

1.1.1.   Non-disclosure Agreement

Before being granted access to classified information, employees must sign Standard Form 312, "Classified Information Nondisclosure Agreement" *(DoD Manual 5200.01, Vol 1, Encl 3, 11.b)*. (See SF 312.) Emphasize the potential damage that may be caused if classified information is mishandled.

1.1.2.   All Personnel

All personnel should be included in initial briefings and provided with a brief explanation of the nature and importance of classified information. They should take the following actions if they discover unsecured classified information:
(DoD Manual 5200.01, Vol 3, Encl 6, 3):

- Take custody of the material
- Safeguard the material
- Immediately notify the security manager or head of the organization
- Notify the next higher level of command or supervisor (if security manager or local head of the activity is presumed to be involved in the compromise)

1.2   DEBRIEFINGS

1.2.1.   With Appropriate Level of Access — Unauthorized Access

If the unauthorized access was by a person with the appropriate level of access but no need-to-know, debriefing is usually appropriate only so far as necessary to ensure the individual is aware of the classified nature of the information and requirement for protection *(DoD Manual 5200.01, Vol 3, Encl 6, 13.a)*.

1.2   DEBRIEFINGS

1.2.2.   Without Appropriate Level of Access — Unauthorized Access

U.S. Government civilian or military personnel or employees of a cleared U.S. Government contractor should be advised of the following:

1.2.3.   Non-DoD and U.S. Government Contractor Employees

Personnel conducting the debriefing must notify the non-DoD and U.S. Government contractor employee's parent organization, to include the Facility Security Officer (FSO), that a debriefing took place *(DoD Manual 5200.01, Vol 3, Encl 6, 13.b)*.

1.2.4.   Statement of Acknowledgement of the Debriefing

The person being debriefed should sign a statement acknowledging the debriefing and his or her understanding of its contents. There is no set format for the statement. If the person refuses to sign a debriefing statement, document the reason and maintain on record for a possible inquiry *(DoD Manual 5200.01, Vol 3, Encl 6, 13.e)*.

1.3   TERMINATION BRIEFING

Each DoD Component must establish its own procedures and format for the termination briefing of cleared employees leaving the organization. Emphasize the employee's responsibility to do the following:

2.1 SECURITY INCIDENTS

These may consist of either security violations or security infractions.

2.1.1. Violations

A violation is any knowing, willful, or negligent action that could reasonably be expected to result in an unauthorized disclosure of classified information. Violations also result if individuals classify or continue the classification of information in violation of an order, create or continue a special access program contrary to the requirements of an order, or contravene any other provision of an order or its implementing directives *(EO 13526)*.

2.1.2. Infractions

An infraction is any knowing, willful, or negligent action contrary to the requirements of an order or its implementing directives that do not comprise a violation, as defined above *(EO 13526)*.

2.1.3. Examples of Security Incidents

Violations:
- Improperly secured classified information
- Open and unattended containers
- Discussing classified information in an unsecured area
- Processing classified information on unclassified automated information systems

Infractions:
- Failure to use a cover sheet
- Not using a security container checklist
- Not using open/closed sign on a security container

2.2 DISCOVERING SECURITY INCIDENTS

Anyone finding classified material out of proper control shall take custody of and safeguard the material, if possible, and immediately notify the appropriate security authorities *(DoD Manual 5200.01, Vol 3, Encl 6, 3.a)*.

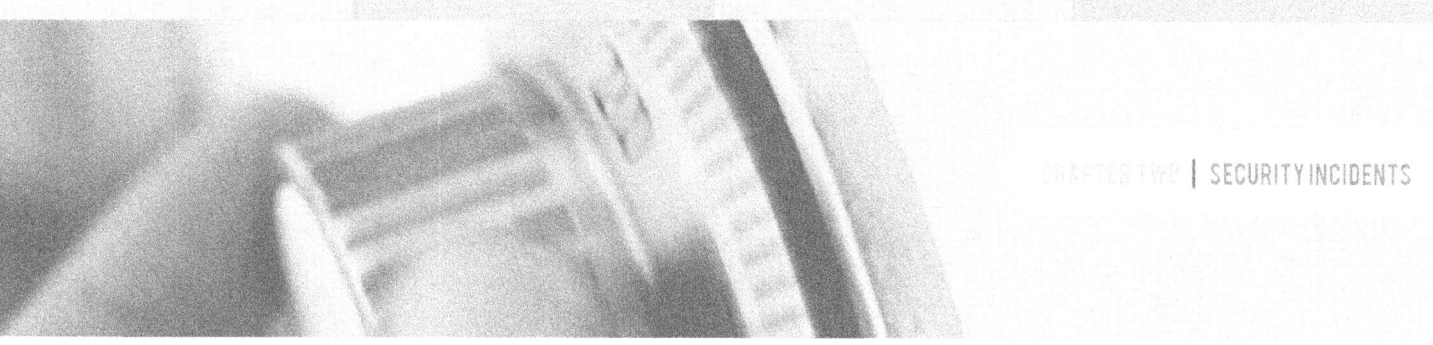

2.3   REPORTING

Any person who becomes aware of the possible compromise of classified information shall immediately report it to the head of his or her local activity or to the activity security manager (*DoD Manual 5200.01, Vol 3, Encl 6, 3.b*).

2.3.1.   Local security officials have specific responsibilities that include the following:

2.3.1.1.   Advise the parent command security organization of compromises occurring within their security cognizance and/or involving personnel assigned to that parent command.

2.3.1.2.   Once confirmed that a potential or actual compromise has occurred and before the conclusion of an inquiry or investigation, notify the originator of the information that a compromise has occurred. The damage assessment is not to be confused either with the classification review performed by the OCA or with damage control actions, which are those actions performed immediately upon the discovery of disclosure or compromise to minimize risk, limit damage, and/or prevent further loss or compromise.

2.3.1.3.   Take prompt action to issue new or revised guidance to correct weaknesses or vulnerabilities in security practices.

2.4   INQUIRY

All security incidents involving classified information shall involve a security inquiry, a security investigation, or both. An inquiry shall be initiated and completed as soon as possible, not to exceed 10 duty days, and a report of finding provided to the activity head, activity security manager, and others as appropriate. When an actual or potential compromise of classified information occurs, the head of the activity or activity security manager, having security knowledge, awareness, and jurisdiction, shall promptly initiate an inquiry into the incident to determine the following (*DoD Manual 5200.01, Vol 3, Encl 6, 3.d*):

2.5 INVESTIGATION

An investigation is conducted for a security violation when the incident cannot be resolved via inquiry or for incidents where an in-depth and comprehensive examination of the matter is required. If the circumstances of an incident are as such that a more detailed investigation is necessary, then an individual will be appointed to conduct that investigation. Appointed individuals:

- Must have a level of access at least equal to the level of the information concerned
- Must have the ability to conduct a thorough and effective investigation
- Must NOT have been involved in the incident
- Should not be the activity security manager, except in unusual circumstances

Individuals appointed to conduct the investigation must do the following:

- Advise their parent command security officials of compromises occurring within their security cognizance and involving personnel assigned to that parent command
- Determine any leads that might identify the person responsible for the compromise
- Determine if further inquiry will increase the damage caused as a result of the compromise

2.6 VERIFICATION, REEVALUATION, & DAMAGE ASSESSMENT

The assessment is to be completed as soon as possible by the original classification authority (OCA) following the immediate notification of the compromise from the activity security manager. The DoD goal for completion of a damage assessment involving compromised classified information is no longer than 6 months from the first date that compromise was declared or 6 months following completion of judicial action (DoD Manual 5200.01, Vol 3, Encl 6, 11).

2.7 DEBRIEFINGS

Refer to DoD Manual 5200.01, Vol 3, Encl 6, 13 for guidance on conducting debriefings.

3.1 ORIGINAL CLASSIFICATION

Original classification is the initial decision that an item of information could reasonably be expected to cause identifiable or describable damage to the national security if subjected to unauthorized disclosure and requires protection in the interest of national security (*DoD Manual 5200.01, Vol 1, Encl 4, Para 4a*).

3.1.1. Original Classification Authority (OCA)
Information may be originally classified in writing by either the President, the Vice President, or by agency heads or other officials designated by the President *(EO 13526)*.

3.1.2. Required Training
All original classification authorities must receive training in proper classification (including the avoidance of over-classification) and declassification as provided in EO 13526 and its implementing directives at least once a calendar year. Such training must include instruction on the proper safeguarding of classified information and on the sanctions in section 5.5 of EO 13526 that may be brought against an individual who fails to classify information properly or protect classified information from unauthorized disclosure. Original classification authorities who do not receive such mandatory training at least once within a calendar year shall have their classification authority suspended by the agency head or the senior agency official designated under section 5.4(d) of EO 13526 until such training has taken place.

3.1.3. Classification Eligibility
Refer to 32 CFR Parts 2001 and 2003 Classified National Security Information: Final Rule, June 2010 and DoD Manual 5200.01, V1, Encl 4, Para. 1.b.

4.1 DERIVATIVE CLASSIFICATION

When incorporating, paraphrasing, restating, or generating classified information in a new form or document (i.e., derivatively classifying information), it must be identified as classified information by marking or similar means. Derivative classification includes classification of information based on classification guidance in a security classification guide or other source material but does not include photocopying or otherwise mechanically or electronically reproducing classified material *(DoD Manual 5200.01, V1, Encl. 4, Para. 10a)*.

4.2 RESPONSIBILITY

No specific delegation of authority is required by persons doing derivative classification. All cleared personnel who generate or create material that should be derivatively classified are responsible for ensuring the derivative classification is accomplished. All persons performing derivative classification shall receive training, as specified in *DoD Manual 5200.01, V3, Encl. 5*, on proper procedures for making classification determinations and properly marking derivatively classified documents. DoD officials who sign or approve derivatively classified documents have principal responsibility for the quality of their derivative classification and must do the following:

- Be identified by name and position, or by personal identifier
- Observe and respect the original classification determination
- Apply appropriate markings
- Use only authorized sources to derivatively classify
- Use caution when paraphrasing or restating extracted information
- Resolve classification conflicts by consulting a SCG or a classified source document (Note: SCG normally takes precedence)
- Receive training in proper application of the derivative classification principles with an emphasis on avoiding over-classification (at least every 2 years)

4.3 AUTHORIZED SOURCES

Authorized sources include Security Classification Guides (SCG), properly marked source material, and DD Form 254 (for contractors).

4.3.1. Procedures for Using Sources Derivative classifiers must do the following:

- Analyze the material to determine any information that contains or reveals classified information
- Appropriately portion mark documents
- Compile a list of sources used and attach to derivative documents
- Carry forward the date or event for declassification that corresponds to the longest period of classification among the sources or markings *(EO 13526)*

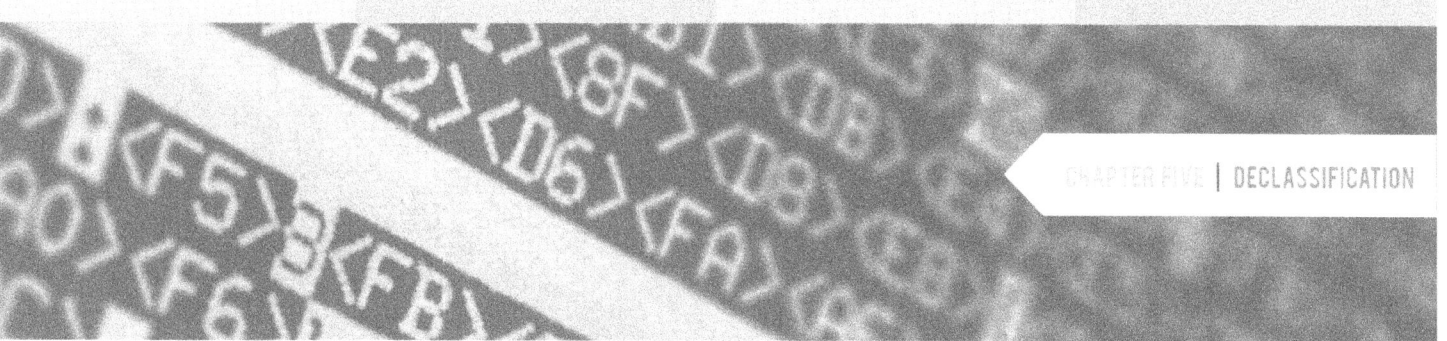

5.1 DECLASSIFICATION

Declassification is the authorized change in the status of information from classified information to unclassified information *(EO 13526)*.

5.2 DECLASSIFICATION GUIDE

A declassification guide contains written instructions issued by a declassification authority that describes the elements of information regarding a specific subject that may be declassified and the elements that must remain classified.

5.3 DECLASSIFICATION SYSTEMS

EO 13526 establishes four separate and parallel systems to declassify information:

5.3.1. Scheduled
The original classifier decides a date or event when information will be declassified.

5.3.2. Automatic
Permanent historical value (PHV) to automatically declassify 25 years from its classification date.

5.3.3. Mandatory
Review for declassification of classified information in response to a request for declassification.

5.3.4. Systematic
A process for review of information for possible declassification of classified information contained in records that have been determined by the Archivist to have permanent historical value in accordance with Title 44, United States Code.

5.4   DECLASSIFICATION AUTHORITY

Information shall be declassified or downgraded by:

- the official who authorized the original classification, if that official is still serving in the same position and has original classification authority
- the originator's current successor in function, if that individual has original classification authority
- a supervisory official of either the originator or his or her successor in function, if the supervisory official has original classification authority
- officials delegated declassification authority in writing by the agency head or the senior agency official of the originating agency

5.4.1.   Declassification Authority

Declassification Authority is not required for simply canceling or changing classification markings in accordance with instructions placed on a document or directions found in a security classification guide or declassification guide.

5.4.2.   Declassification Options

Information may be declassified using one of the following schedules:

- A date or event 10 years from origination
- A date or event up to 25 years
- 25X1 through 25X9, with a date or event
- 50X1–HUM or 50X2–WMD, or Information Security Oversight Office (ISOO)-approved designator reflecting the Panel approval for classification beyond 50 years. Agencies have the authority to use "50X1–HUM" without requesting specific authorization from the Interagency Security Classification Appeals Panel; however, agencies are required to cite their intention to use this marking in their declassification guides.
- Absent guidance from an original classification authority with jurisdiction over the information, a calculated 25-year date from the date of the source document

6.1   OVERALL CLASSIFICATION MARKING RULES

All classified information shall be clearly identified by electronic labeling, designation or marking. Classification markings must be conspicuous. Classified documents must be marked with the highest classification of information it contains. If physical marking of the medium containing classified information is not possible, then identification of classified information must be accomplished by other means (*DoD Manual 5200.01, Vol. 2, Encl. 3, Para. 1*).

6.2   CLASSIFIED DOCUMENTS MARKING REQUIREMENTS

Must bear the following markings:

6.2.1.	Banner markings must be marked on the top and bottom of the front page or title page and outside back cover (if any). Internal pages may be marked with the banner markings of the document or the highest classification of the information contained on that page.
6.2.2.	The Agency and office of origin
6.2.3.	Date of origin
6.2.4.	"Classified by" for original and derivatively classified documents; "(Name and Position)"
6.2.5.	Reason (original classification only)
6.2.6.	"Derived from" line for derivatively classified documents; "(List Sources)"
6.2.7.	Declassification instructions. YYYYMMDD format
6.2.8.	Downgrading instructions, if applicable
6.2.9.	Portion Markings
6.2.10.	Dissemination Control notices (front page)

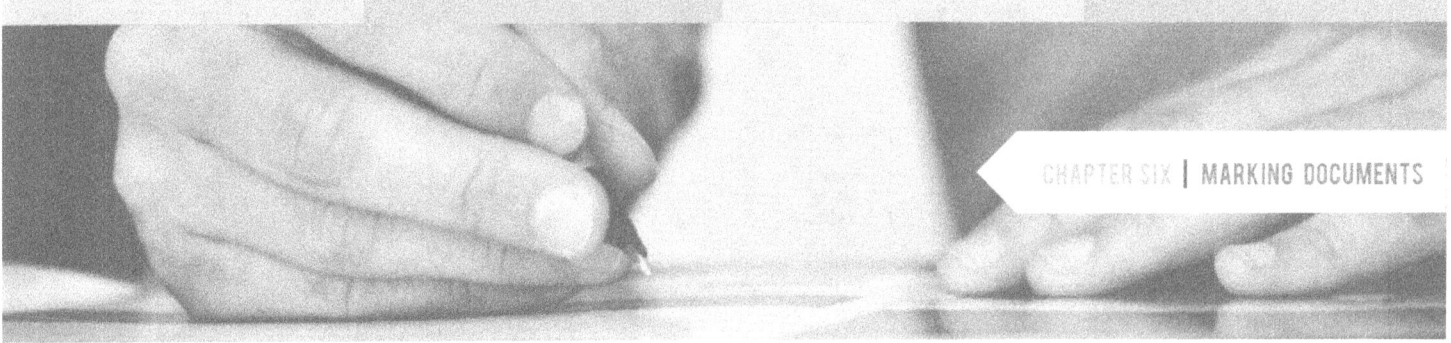

Example: Originally Classified

> SECRET
> ON-SITE INSPECTION AGENCY
> Umatilla Army Depot Field Office
> Umatilla, Oregon 97882-6001
>
> December 02, 2011
>
> ABC-OD
> Subject: (U) Sarinwind Project
>
> 1. (S) Everything about Sarinwind locations is now declassified. The fact that Sarinwind is highly lethal is still classified Secret.
>
> 2. (U) POC for this memo is Randy Travis, DSN 222-4888.
>
> Classified by: Randy Travis, Ops Dir, 504 MIB
> Reason: 1.4c, Crypto systems
> Downgrade on: 20130115
> Declassify on: 25X3, 20611221
>
> SECRET
> (Unclassified-marked classified for training purposes only)

Example: Derivatively Classified

> SECRET
> ON-SITE INSPECTION AGENCY
> Umatilla Army Depot Field Office
> Umatilla, Oregon 97882-6001
>
> December 02, 2011
>
> ABC-OD
> Subject: (U) Sarinwind Project
>
> 1. (S) Everything about Sarinwind locations is now declassified. The fact that Sarinwind is highly lethal is still classified Secret.
>
> 2. (U) POC for this memo is Randy Travis, DSN 222-4888.
>
> Classified by: Randy Travis, Ops Dir, 504 MIB
> Derived from: Multiple Sources (Listed on last page)
> Downgrade on: 20130115
> Declassify on: 25X3, 20611221
>
> SECRET
> (Unclassified-marked classified for training purposes only)

6.3   ORIGINALLY CLASSIFIED DOCUMENTS

Every originally classified document must have a "Classified by" line placed on the face of the document that identifies the OCA responsible for classification of the information it contains. The OCA shall be identified by name and position title or personal identifier (*DoD Manual 5200.01, Vol. 2, Encl. 3, Para. 8.b*).

6.3.1.   Reason for Classification

Each originally classified document shall bear a concise statement of the reason for classification determined by the original classifier in accordance with EO 13526.

6.4   DERIVATIVELY CLASSIFIED DOCUMENTS

Derivatively classified documents shall be marked with a "Classified by" line identifying, by name and position or identifier, the person performing the derivative classification *(E. O. 13526)*.

6.4.1.   "Derived from" line

If more than one security classification guide (SCG), source document, or combination of these are used, place "Multiple Sources" on the "Derived from" line and attach a listing of all sources used *(EO 13526)*.

6.5   DECLASSIFICATION INSTRUCTIONS

Every classified document must have a Classification Authority Box *(DoD Manual 5200.01, Vol 2, Encl 3, Para. 8.b.1.d)*.

6.6   TENTATIVE CLASSIFICATION

Individuals who submit information to OCAs for original classification decisions shall provide the OCA the information required by DoD Manual 5200.01, V1, Encl. 4, Para. 6.a. through 6.f, and may, as necessary, tentatively classify information or documents as working papers, pending approval by the OCA. Final classification decisions must be made as soon as possible, but not later than 180 days from the initial drafting date of the document. Prior to the OCA's classification decision, such information shall be safeguarded as required for the specified level of classification and it shall not be used as a source for derivative classification.

7.1   POLICY

Components must have a system of control measures appropriate to the environment where access to classified information occurs. Classified information must be protected at all times either by storage in an approved device or facility or having it under the personal observation and control of an authorized individual. The system must include technical, physical, and personnel control measures. Several control measures are listed below *(DoD Manual 5200.01, V3, Encl. 2, Para. 1)*.

7.2   STANDARD FORMS

The Standard Form 700 Series is mandated for use for all departments and independent agencies or offices that create and/or handle national security information. These forms serve the purpose of providing identification, control, and safeguarding of classified and sensitive information.

These forms are listed below:

- Standard Form 700 – Security Container Information
- Standard Form 701 – End of Day Checklist
- Standard Form 702 – Security Container Check Sheet
- Standard Form 703 – Top Secret Cover Sheet
- Standard Form 704 – Secret Cover Sheet
- Standard Form 705 – Confidential Cover Sheet
- Standard Form 706 – Top Secret Label
- Standard Form 707 – Secret Label
- Standard Form 708 – Confidential Label
- Standard Form 709 – Classified Label
- Standard Form 710 – Unclassified Label
- Standard Form 711 – Data Descriptor Label

7.2   STANDARD FORMS

7.2.1.   SF 700

provides the names, addresses and telephone numbers of employees who are to be contacted if the security container to which the form pertains is found open and unattended. The form also includes the means to maintain a current record of the security container's combination and provides the envelope to be used to forward this information to the appropriate agency activity or official. The national stock number for the SF 700 is 7540–01–214–5372.

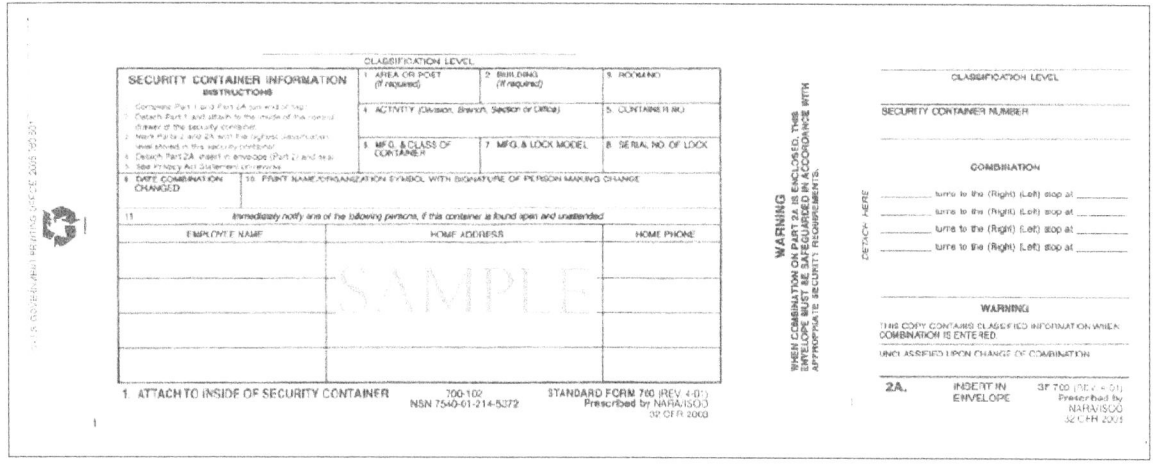

7.2.2.   SF 701

provides a systematic means to make a thorough end-of-day security inspection for a particular work area and to allow for employee accountability in the event irregularities are discovered. The national stock number for the SF 701 is 7540–01–213–7899.

7.2 STANDARD FORMS

7.2.3. SF 702

provides a record of the names and times persons have opened, closed and checked a particular container that holds classified information. The national stock number of the SF 702 is 7540–01–213–7900.

7.2.4. SF 703

serves as a shield to protect TOP SECRET classified information from inadvertent disclosure and to alert observers that TOP SECRET information is attached to it. SF 703 is affixed to the top of the TOP SECRET document and remains attached until the document is destroyed or secured in a GSA security container authorized to store TOP SECRET information. At the time of destruction, SF 703 is removed and, depending upon its condition, reused. The national stock number of the SF 703 is 7540–01–213–7901.

7.2.5. SF 704

serves as a shield to protect SECRET classified information from inadvertent disclosure and to alert observers that SECRET information is attached to it. SF 704 is affixed to the top of the SECRET document and remains attached until the document is destroyed or secured in a GSA security container authorized to store SECRET information. At the time of destruction, SF 704 is removed and, depending upon its condition, reused. The national stock number of the SF 704 is 7540–01–213–7902.

7.2 STANDARD FORMS

7.2.6. SF 705

serves as a shield to protect CONFIDENTIAL classified information from inadvertent disclosure and to alert observers that CONFIDENTIAL information is attached to it. SF 705 is affixed to the top of the CONFIDENTIAL document and remains attached until the document is destroyed or secured in a GSA security container authorized to store CONFIDENTIAL information. At the time of destruction, SF 705 is removed and, depending upon its condition, reused. The national stock number for the SF 705 is 7540–01–213–7903.

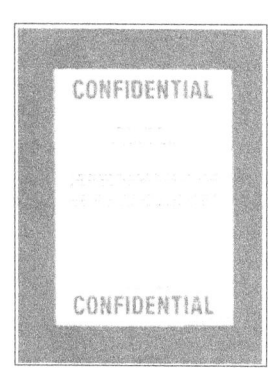

7.2.7. SF 706

is used to identify and protect automatic data processing (ADP) media and other media containing TOP SECRET information. SF 706 is used instead of the SF 703 for media other than documents. SF 706 is affixed to the medium containing TOP SECRET information in a manner that would not adversely affect operation of equipment in which the medium is used. Once the label has been applied, it cannot be removed. The national stock number of the SF 706 is 7540–01–207–5536.

7.2.8. SF 707

is used to identify and protect automatic data processing (ADP) media and other media containing SECRET information. SF 707 is used instead of the SF 704 for media other than documents. SF 707 is affixed to the medium containing SECRET information in a manner that would not adversely affect operation of equipment in which the medium is used. Once the label has been applied, it cannot be removed. The national stock number of the SF 707 is 7540–01–207–5537.

7.2   STANDARD FORMS

7.2.9.   SF 708

is used to identify and protect automatic data processing (ADP) media and other media containing CONFIDENTIAL information. SF 706 is used instead of the SF 703 for media other than documents. SF 706 is affixed to the medium containing CONFIDENTIAL information in a manner that would not adversely affect operation of equipment in which the medium is used. Once the label has been applied, it cannot be removed. The national stock number of the SF 708 is 7540–01–207–5536.

7.2.10.   SF 709

is used to identify and protect electronic media and other media that contain classified information pending a determination by the classifier of the specific classification level of the information. The SF 709 is affixed to the medium containing classified information in a manner that would not adversely affect operation of equipment in which the medium is used. Once the label has been applied, it cannot be removed. When a classifier has made a determination of the specific level of classification of the information contained on the medium, either, SF 706, SF 707, or SF 708 shall be affixed on top of SF 709 so that only the SF 706, SF 707, or SF 708 is visible. The national stock number of the SF 709 is 7540 01–207–5540.

7.2 STANDARD FORMS

7.2.11. SF 710

In a mixed environment in which classified and unclassified information are being processed or stored, SF 710 is used to identify automatic data processing (ADP) media and other media containing unclassified information. Its function is to aid in distinguishing among those media that contain either classified or unclassified information in a mixed environment. Only the Director of the Information Security Oversight Office (ISOO) may grant a waiver from the use of SF 710. The national stock number of the SF 710 is 7540–01–207–5539.

This medium is

UNCLASSIFIED

U.S. Government Property
SF 710 (1-87)

7.2.12. SF 711

is used to identify additional safeguarding controls that pertain to classified information stored or contained on automatic data processing (ADP) or other media. SF 711 shall be used in all situations requiring the use of a DATA DESCRIPTOR label. SF 711 is affixed to the ADP medium containing classified information in a manner that would not adversely affect operation of equipment in which the medium is used. SF 711 is ordinarily used in conjunction with the SF 706, SF 707, SF 708 or SF 709, as appropriate. The national stock number of the SF 711 is 7540–01–207–5541.

(picture not available)

7.3 STORAGE

Classified information must be secured under conditions adequate to prevent access by unauthorized persons. GSA establishes and publishes minimum standards, specifications, and supply schedules for containers, vault doors, modular vaults, alarm systems, and associated security devices suitable for the storage and protection of classified information.

7.3.1. Military and Military Support

The Heads of DoD Components shall delineate the appropriate security measures required to protect classified information stored in containers on military platforms or for classified munitions items as long as they are consistent with DoD Manual 5200.01.

7.3.2. Field Safes

GSA-approved field safes and special size one- and two-drawer security containers approved by the GSA may be used for storage of classified information in the field and in military platforms. These containers shall use locks meeting Underwriters Laboratories Inc. Standard 768, Group I or Federal Specification FF-L-2937. Special size containers shall be securely fastened to the platform; field safes shall be under sufficient control and surveillance when in use to prevent unauthorized access or loss.

7.3.3. Map and Plan Files

GSA-approved map and plan files are used to store irregular sized items such as computer media, maps, charts, and classified equipment. These files should be securely fastened to a structure or under sufficient surveillance to prevent their theft.

7.3.4. Bulky Material

Storage areas for bulky material containing Secret or Confidential information may have access openings (e.g., roof hatches, vents) secured by GSA-approved changeable combination padlocks meeting Federal Specification FF-P-110. Other security measures are required, in accordance with paragraphs 3.b. and 3.c. of this enclosure.

7.3.4.1. Exception

Heads of DoD Components may authorize the use of key-operated locks for the storage of Secret and Confidential information when special circumstances exist. The authorization shall be documented with an explanation of the special circumstances that warrant deviation from other established standards Additional administrative procedures must be used to account for, control, and protect the keys and locks at the equivalent level of the classified information.

7.3.5. Modular Vaults

As an alternative to using vaults, GSA-approved modular vaults must meet Federal Specification AA-V-2737 and may be used to store classified information. Listed in the chart below are products qualified under Federal Specification AA-V-2737 (QPL-AA-V-2737-5, October 17, 2007, www.gsa.gov).

7.3   STORAGE

7.3.5.   Modular Vaults

Government Designation	Manufacturer's Designation (Brand Name)	Test or Qualification Reference Number	Manufacturer's Name
Type I – Lightweight Style A – Six-sided	Class 5	3FNE-93-169	Modular Vault Systems, Inc. 832 Oregon Avenue Suite H-J Linthicum, MD 21090 Plant: Same address
Type II – Heavyweight Style A – Six-sided	17306	D/M-MV-307	Diebold Incorporated 818 Mulberry Road SE Canton, OH 44707-3256 Plant: Lindsay Concrete Products, Inc. 6845 Erie Avenue PO Box 578 Canal Fulton, OH 44614 And following subsidiaries: Southern Precast, Inc. 13365 Southern Precast Drive Alachua, FL 32615
Type II – Heavyweight Style B – Five-sided	17305	D/M-MV-307	Firebaugh Pre-cast, Inc. PO Box 5440 Colorado Springs, CO 80931 Stay-Right Precast, Inc. 2675 U.S. 1 Highway PO Box 580 Franklinton, NC 27525
Type I – Lightweight Style A – Six-sided	Class 5	3FNE-93-184	Plant: International Vault, Inc. 54 Danbury Road. Suite 369 Ridgefield, CT 06877
Type II – Heavyweight Style A – Six-sided	Mega Crete MMV-6	I-MV-1007	Plant: International Vault, Inc. 2469 Old Route 421 North Siler City, NC 27344
Type II – Heavyweight Style B – Five-sided	Mega Crete MMV-5	I-MV-1007	Plant: International Vault, Inc. 2469 Old Route 421 North Siler City, NC 27344

7.3 STORAGE

7.3.6. Top Secret

Top Secret information must be stored by one of the following methods:

7.3.6.1. Field Conditions / Military Operations

Under field conditions during military operations, using such storage devices or security control measures as a military commander deems adequate to prevent unauthorized access. Military commanders should employ risk management methodologies when determining appropriate safeguards (DoD Manual 5200.01, V3, Para 3.a.5).

7.3.6.2. Supplementary Controls

In a GSA-approved container with at least one supplemental control measure, i.e., continuous protection by a cleared guard, a cleared guard must inspect container once every 2 hours; protected by an intrusion detection system (IDS), with personnel responding to the alarm arriving within 15 minutes; Security-In-Depth when the GSA-approved container is equipped with a lock meeting Federal Specifications FF-L-2740 (some common locks meeting this specification are the X0-7, X0-8, X0-9, CDX-07, CDX-08, CDX-09).

7.3.6.3. Vaults

Vaults must be equipped with an Intrusion Detection System (IDS) with personnel responding to the alarm within 15 minutes if the area is covered by Security-In-Depth or 5 minutes if not covered by Security-In-Depth. Vault walls must be 8" thick reinforced concrete. Vault roofs must be at least 8" monolithic concrete, and vault frame and doors must be of Class 5 or Class 8 construction.

7.3.6.4. Secure Room

The walls, floor, and roof construction of secure rooms must be of permanent construction materials; i.e., plaster, gypsum wallboard, metal panels, hardboard, wood, plywood, or other materials offering resistance to and evidence of unauthorized entry into the area. Walls shall be extended to the true ceiling and attached with permanent construction materials, with mesh or 18-gauge expanded steel screen. The access door to the room shall be substantially constructed of wood or metal. The hinge pins of out-swing doors shall be pinned, brazed, or spot welded to prevent removal. Door should be equipped with a built-in GSA-approved combination lock meeting Federal Specification FF-L-2740. Windows measured from the bottom must be less than 18 feet from the ground. If they are fewer than 18 feet from the ground, they must be covered by material that will provide protection against forced entry.

7.3   STORAGE

7.3.7.   Secret

Secret information must be stored by one of the following methods:

7.3.7.1.   Field Conditions / Military Operations

Under field conditions during military operations, using such storage devices or security control measures as a military commander deems adequate to prevent unauthorized access. Military commanders should employ risk management methodologies when determining appropriate safeguards.

7.3.7.2.   Supplementary Controls

In a GSA-approved container or vault without supplemental controls.

7.3.7.3.   Secure Rooms

Secure rooms approved for storage of Secret information prior to October 1, 1995, are subject to continuous protection by a cleared guard; a cleared guard must inspect the security container once every 4 hours, or an IDS must be installed with personnel responding within 30 minutes of the alarm.

7.3.7.4.   Open Storage

In an open storage area meeting the requirements of the DoD Manual 5200.01, provided the senior agency official determines that Security-In-Depth exists and one of the following supplemental controls is utilized:

a.   The location that houses the container shall be subject to continuous protection by cleared guard or duty personnel.

b.   Cleared guard or duty personnel shall inspect the security container once every 4 hours.

c.   An IDS meeting the requirements of the Manual, with the personnel responding to the alarm arriving within 30 minutes of the alarm.

The DoD Component must reassess the requirement for the secure room and makes plans to bring the room up to the standards of subparagraphs DoDM 5200.01-V3, Encl. 3, 3.b.(1) through 3.b.(3) by October 1, 2013, and provided the area has been determined to have Security-In-Depth.

7.3 STORAGE

7.3.8. Confidential

Confidential information must be stored in the same manner as prescribed for Top Secret or Secret information except that supplemental controls are not required.

7.3.9. Weapons and Sensitive Items

Weapons, ammunitions, and explosives and items such as funds, jewels, precious metals, or drugs/medication must not be stored in the same container used to safeguard classified information.

7.3.10. Sensitive Compartmented Information Facilities (SCIFs)

All Intelligence Community (IC) SCIFs shall comply with uniform IC physical and technical security requirements. Intelligence Community Directive (ICD) 705 and Intelligence Community Standard (ICS) Number 705-1, which is designed to ensure the protection of Sensitive Compartmented Information (SCI) and foster efficient, consistent, and reciprocal use of SCIFs in the IC. This Directive applies to all facilities accredited by IC elements where SCI is processed, stored, used, or discussed.

7.4 INFORMATION DATA PROCESSING (IDP) AND AUTOMATED DATA PROCESSING (ADP) EQUIPMENT

The National Security Agency (NSA) establishes the minimum standards and specifications for information data processing equipment. The Department of Defense has a variety of non-COMSEC-approved equipment used to process classified information. Activities must identify those features, parts, or functions of equipment used to process classified information and properly label them to prevent unauthorized access. It is mandatory to use the SF 706 (Top Secret), SF 707 (Secret), SF 708 (Confidential), SF 709 (Classified) and SF 710 (Unclassified) labels to satisfy this requirement.

8.1 CONTROLLED UNCLASSIFIED INFORMATION

Controlled Unclassified Information (CUI) includes For Official Use Only (FOUO) information, Sensitive but Unclassified (SBU) information, and DEA Sensitive Information (DSEN). This is not an all-inclusive list. See DoDM 5200.01, Volume 4 to review the requirements and released guidance regarding unclassified information designations.

8.1.1. Markings

FOUO, SBU, and DSEN have different requirements for marking.

8.1.1.1. FOUO

Paper documents containing FOUO information must be marked on the bottom of the front cover (if there is one), the title page (if there is one), the first page, and the outside of the back cover (if there is one), and any internal pages of the document containing FOUO with "FOR OFFICIAL USE ONLY".

8.1.1.1.1. Other Material Containing FOUO

Materials other than paper (i.e. slides, computer media, films, etc.) must be marked appropriately to alert the holder or viewer that the material contains FOUO information.

8.1.1.2. SBU

Within the Department of Defense, the criteria for allowing access to SBU information are the same as those used for FOUO information, EXECPT that information marked "SBU NOFORN" (or portion marked "(SBU-NF)") shall not be provided to any person who is not a U.S. citizen without the approval of the DoS activity that originated the information.

8.1.1.3. DSEN

DEA Sensitive information is unclassified information that the DEA originates and that requires protection against unauthorized disclosure to protect sources and methods of investigative activity, evidence, and the integrity of pretrial investigative reports. The Administrator and certain other officials of the DEA have been authorized to designate information as DEA Sensitive; the Department of Defense agreed to implement protective measures for DEA Sensitive information in its possession. Types of information to be protected include:

a. Information and material that is investigative in nature.

b. Information and material to which access is restricted by law.

c. Information and material that is critical to the operation and mission of the DEA.

d. Information and material the disclosure of which would violate a privileged relationship.

8.1   CONTROLLED UNCLASSIFIED INFORMATION

8.1.1.3.1.   **DSEN Markings**

a. Unclassified documents containing DEA Sensitive information shall be marked "DEA SENSITIVE" at the top and bottom of the front cover (if there is one), the title page (if there is one), the first page, and the outside of the back cover (if there is one) and each page containing DEA Sensitive information shall be marked "DEA SENSITIVE" top and bottom. Portions of unclassified DoD documents that contain DEA Sensitive information shall be marked with the parenthetical notation "(DSEN)" at the beginning of the portion.

b. Classified documents containing DEA Sensitive information shall be marked in accordance with Volume 2 of the manual. Pages containing DEA Sensitive information but no classified information may be marked "UNCLASSIFIED// DEA SENSITIVE" top and bottom. If a portion of a classified document contains DEA Sensitive information, include the "DSEN" marking after the parenthetical classification marking (e.g., (U//DSEN)). Classified and DEA Sensitive portions should be kept separate.

8.1.1.3.2.   **DSEN Access**

Access to DEA Sensitive information shall be granted only to persons who have a valid need-to-know for the information. A security clearance is not required for access to unclassified DEA Sensitive information. DEA Sensitive information in the possession of the Department of Defense may not be released outside the Department without DEA authorization.

a. (DEA Sensitive material may be transmitted within the continental United States (CONUS) by first class mail. Transmission outside CONUS shall be by a means approved for transmission of Secret material. Non-government package delivery and courier services may not be used. Enclose the material in two opaque envelopes or containers, the inner one marked "DEA SENSITIVE" on both sides.

8.1   CONTROLLED UNCLASSIFIED INFORMATION

b.   Electronic transmission of DEA Sensitive information within CONUS shall be over secure communications circuits whenever possible; electronic transmission outside CONUS shall be over approved secure communications circuits.

c.   Reproduction of DEA Sensitive information and material shall be limited to that required for operational needs.

d.   DEA Sensitive material shall be destroyed by a means approved for destruction of material classified Confidential.

8.1.2.   Protection

FOUO, SBU, and DSEN must be protected in the best interest of national security.

8.1.2.1.   FOUO

During work hours, take steps to minimize access by unauthorized personnel. After work hours, secure material in locked desks, file cabinets, bookcases, locked rooms, or similar items. However, if stored where Government or Government contract building security is provided, the FOUO information may be stored in unlocked containers, desks, or cabinets.

8.1.2.2.   SBU

Protect in the same manner as FOUO information.

8.1.2.3.   DSEN

DEA Sensitive material may be transmitted within the continental United States (CONUS) by first class mail. Transmission outside CONUS shall be by a means approved for transmission of Secret material. Non-government package delivery and courier services may not be used. Enclose the material in two opaque envelopes or containers, the inner one marked "DEA SENSITIVE" on both sides.

9.1 ENVELOPES OR CONTAINERS

Classified information must be double-wrapped using two opaque, sealed envelopes with the wrappings or containers being durable enough to properly protect the material.

9.1.1. Internal Classified Components
The outside shell or body of the packageable items or equipment may be used as the inner wrapping if it does not reveal classified information.

9.1.2. Irregular Bulky Items
Must be covered with an opaque cover if the shell or body of the item reveals classified features.

9.1.3. Specialized Containers
May be considered the outer wrapping or cover.

9.1.4. Briefcases
If classified material is transported outside of the activity, a locked briefcase may serve as the outer wrapper.

9.1.5. NATO Restricted Material
This material does not need to be double-wrapped when transmitted within the United States. The marking "NATO Restricted" must not appear on the wrapper.

9.1.6. Classified Text
Wrap documents so the classified text is not in direct contact with the inner envelope or container.

9.2 ADDRESSING

Properly wrapped classified information must be addressed to an official Government activity or DoD contractor with a facility clearance and appropriate storage capability.

9.2.1. Outer Envelope or Container
Shall not be addressed to an individual and must show the complete return address of the sender. Office codes or phrases such as "Attention: Center for Development of Security Excellence" may be used.

9.2.2. Inner Envelope or Container
The inner envelope or container may have an attention line listing the recipient's name. The inner envelope or container must show the address of the receiving activity, the address of the sender, and the highest classification of the contents, including any special markings, such as "Restricted Data."

9.2.3. U.S. Elements of International Staffs
The information must be addressed specifically to those elements.

10.1   POLICY

Head of the DoD Components must establish procedures to minimize the risk of compromise of classified information and utilize the most cost effective method of transmitting or transporting the classified information.

10.1.1.   Dissemination

Allows classified information from one agency to be provided to another agency or U.S. entity, without the consent of the originating agency, unless the originating agency has required prior authorization and has marked the information accordingly.

10.2   TOP SECRET INFORMATION

Top Secret information must only be transmitted as listed below:

10.3 SECRET INFORMATION

Secret information may be transmitted as listed below:

- Any method approved to transmit or transport Top Secret information

- Appropriately cleared contractor employees

- On exception basis under urgent requirements, Agency Heads may authorize overnight delivery to a DoD Component within the U.S. and its territories by a GSA contract holder. The sender is responsible for ensuring that an authorized person will be available to receive the delivery. The release signature block shall not be used under any circumstances.

- Registered mail within the U.S., District of Columbia, and Commonwealth of Puerto Rico

- Registered mail through the Army, Navy, or Air Force Postal Service facilities outside the U.S. and its territories, although it must remain in the control of U.S. citizens

- Registered mail between the U.S. Postal Service and Canadian service with registered mail receipt

- Express mail within the U.S., the District of Columbia, and Commonwealth of Puerto Rico. The sender cannot use street-side Express mail collection boxes. The information cannot be delivered without a signature.

- Carriers cleared under the National Industrial Security program (NISP) who provide a Protective Security Service within CONUS

10.4 CONFIDENTIAL INFORMATION

Confidential information may be transmitted as listed below:

11.1. AUTHORIZED HANDCARRY PROVISIONS

Appropriately cleared personnel may be authorized to escort or hand-carry classified material to the highest level of access possessed by the individual between locations if other means of transmission or transportation cannot be used.

11.2. FOREIGN CARRIER

Hand-carrying classified information is authorized on a foreign flagged carrier if no U.S. carrier is available; however, the classified information will remain in the custody and physical control of the U.S. escort at all times.

11.3. DISCLOSURE TO FOREIGN NATIONALS

DoD Component officials responsible for approving the hand-carry are responsible for ensuring disclosure authorization has been obtained if the classified information will be disclosed to foreign nationals.

11.4. STORAGE

If storage is required, arrangements for secure storage must be made at a U.S. Government or cleared U.S. contractor facility.

11.5. COURIER RESPONSIBILITIES

Couriers must be informed of and acknowledge their security responsibilities. The courier may be briefed or read written instructions and acknowledge the understanding and compliance to the requirements listed below:

- The courier is liable and responsible for the material being escorted.
- The classified material will not be left unattended.
- During overnight stops, classified materials will be stored in a U.S. military facility, embassies or consulates, or cleared U.S. contractor facilities.
- Classified material shall not be stored in hotel safes.
- Classified material shall not be discussed or disclosed in public.
- The courier shall not deviate from the authorized travel schedule.
- The courier must take measures to protect classified material in the event of an emergency situation.

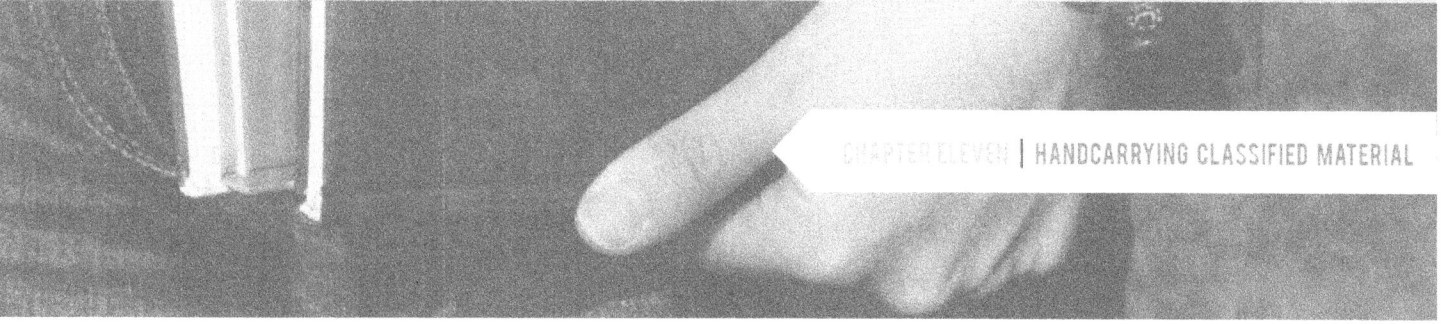
11.5. COURIER RESPONSIBILITIES

There is no assurance of immunity from search by customs, police, and/or immigration officials. The courier must adhere to the following instructions:

11.6. DOCUMENTATION

Responsible officials must provide a written authorization statement to all individuals escorting or carrying classified material. The authorization statement may be included in official travel orders, except for travel aboard commercial aircraft.

"Courier Authorization" (DD Form 2501) may be used to identify appropriately cleared DoD military and civilian personnel who have been approved to handcarry classified material except for aboard commercial aircraft. Use the DD Form 2501 as listed below:

- The courier has a need to hand-carry classified information recurrently.

- An appropriate official in the courier's security office signs the form.

- Forms are controlled to prevent unauthorized use.

- The form is issued for only 2 years at a time.

- The form may be used for identification/verification of authorization to handcarry Sensitive Compartment Information (SCI) or Special Access Program (SAP) information in accordance to the policies and procedures established by the security officer responsible for the program.

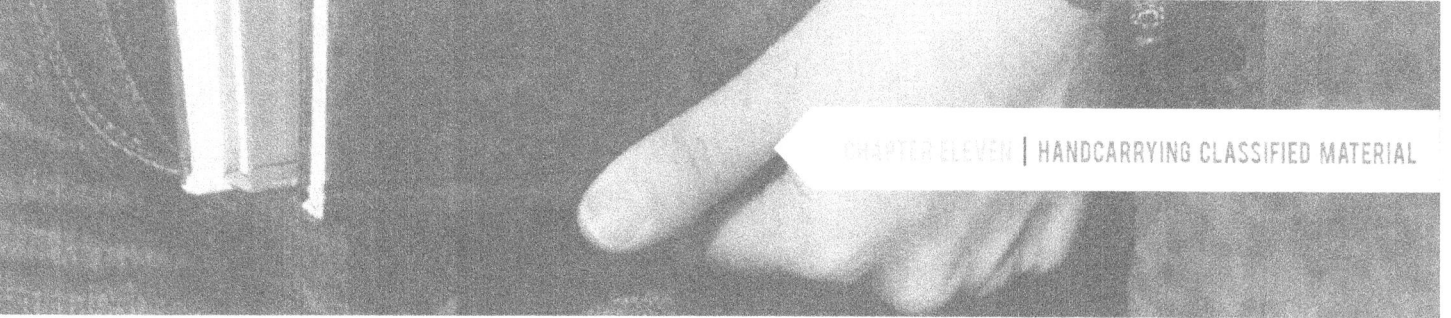

11.7. COMMERCIAL PASSENGER AIRCRAFT

Couriers must possess a DoD or contractor issued identification card which includes a photograph, descriptive data, and signature of the courier.

11.7.1. To facilitate processing classified information through commercial airline ticketing, screening, and boarding procedures and verifying documentation that will be required, advance coordination should be undertaken with airline security and Transportation Security Administration (TSA).

The individual designated as courier shall possess a DoD or contractor-issued identification card and a government-issued photo identification card. (If at least one of the identification cards does not contain date of birth, height, weight, and signature, include these items in the written authorization.)

11.7.2. The courier shall have the original authorization letter and sufficient authenticated copies to provide at each screening point. The letter, prepared on letterhead stationary of the agency authorizing the carrying of classified material, shall:

11.7.3. The courier shall go through the same airline ticketing and boarding process as other passengers. When the TSA Supervisory Transportation Security Officer confirms the courier's authorization to carry classified material, only the U.S. Government classified material is exempted from any form of inspection; the courier and all of the courier's personal property shall be provided for screening. When requested, the package(s) or the carry-on luggage containing the classified information may be presented for security screening so long as the courier maintains visual sight and the packaging or luggage is not opened.

12.1. POLICY

Classified documents and material identified for destruction shall be destroyed completely, to prevent anyone from reconstructing the classified information, according to procedures and methods the DoD Component Head or designee prescribes. Methods and equipment used to routinely destroy classified information include burning, crosscut shredding, wet pulping, mutilation, chemical decomposition or pulverizing.

At a minimum, the volume and content of each activity's classified material destruction flow shall be assessed and a process established to optimize the use of high security crosscut paper shredders (i.e., with top secret collateral material being the highest collateral priority) to take full advantage of the added security value of those shredders. The bag of shred must be "stirred" to ensure the content is mixed up. Shredding of unclassified material along with the classified material is encouraged.

12.2. ANNUAL "CLEAN OUT DAY"

Each activity with classified information shall establish at least one day within each year to focus on the disposal of unneeded classified information.

12.3. ADDITIONAL TECHNIQUES TO REDUCE HOLDINGS

Activities should establish techniques or standard operating procedures to reduce classified holdings. Some techniques are listed below:

- Schedule Inquiries – if an activity has a lot of material on hand, schedule an inquiry to see if the material is being used in a timely manner.

- Create Review Sheets – a review sheet is given to the office of primary responsibility to determine whether the material is still required.

- Conduct random checks to verify material requirement and/or use.

- Conduct self-inspections with reports.

- Consolidate holdings whenever possible. Make sure to not mix classified materials requiring additional controls and protective measures, i.e., NATO, SAP, and COMSEC.

12.4. AUTHORIZED DESTRUCTION

The following personnel are authorized to destroy classified information: OCAs, derivative classifiers, custodian or users; individuals designated by heads of activities; specified control officers such as NATO, COMSEC, or Top Secret Control Officers (TSCO).

13.1. PUBLIC LAWS, STATUTES & EXECUTIVE ORDERS

a. Executive Order 10964, "Safeguarding Official Information in the Interest of the Defense of the United States," September 21, 1961.

b. Executive Order 12065, "National Security Information," June 28, 1978.

c. Executive Order 12333, "United States Intelligence Activities," December 4, 1981.

d. Executive Order 12356, "National Security Information," April 2, 1982.

e. Executive Order 13526, "Classified National Security Information," December 29, 2009.

f. Executive Order 13556, "Controlled Unclassified Information," November 4, 2010.

13.2. DOD DIRECTIVES, INSTRUCTIONS & MANUALS

a. DoD Manual 5200.01, Volumes 1-4, "DoD Information Security Program," February 24, 2012.

b. DoD 5200.2-R, "DoD Personnel Security Program Regulation," January 1987.

c. DoD Instruction 5200.33, "Defense Courier Service Instruction," June 30, 2011.

d. DoD 5220.22-M, "National Industrial Security Program Operating Manual," January 1995 and its supplements.

e. DoD 5220.22-R, "Industrial Security Regulation," December 1985.

13.3. OTHER GUIDANCE

a. 32 CFR Parts 2001 and 2003 Classified National Security Information; Final Rule, June 28, 2010.

b. Information Security Oversight Office Marking Booklet, Revision 1, January 2012.